profit + impact

Copyright © 2018 Daniela Gabrielle Smallwood

All rights reserved.

ISBN: 1979476535
ISBN-13: 9781979476539

i am bursting with EXTRAORDINARILY profitable + impactful STRATEGIES, ideas, & SOLUTIONS

profit + impact

everything i touch profits

profit + impact

everything i touch profits

profit + impact

everything i touch profits

profit + impact

everything i touch profits

profit + impact

everything i touch profits

profit + impact

everything i touch profits

profit + impact

everything i touch profits

profit + impact

everything i touch profits

profit + impact

everything i touch profits

profit + impact

everything i touch profits

profit + impact

everything i touch profits

profit + impact

everything i touch profits

profit + impact

everything i touch profits

profit + impact

everything i touch profits

profit + impact

everything i touch profits

profit + impact

everything i touch profits

profit + impact

everything i touch profits

profit + impact

everything i touch profits

profit + impact

everything i touch profits

profit + impact

everything i touch profits

profit + impact

everything i touch profits

profit + impact

everything i touch profits

profit + impact

everything i touch profits

profit + impact

everything i touch profits

profit + impact

everything i touch profits

profit + impact

everything i touch profits

profit + impact

everything i touch profits

profit + impact

everything i touch profits

profit + impact

everything i touch profits

profit + impact

everything i touch profits

profit + impact

everything i touch profits

profit + impact

everything i touch profits

profit + impact

everything i touch profits

profit + impact

everything i touch profits

profit + impact

everything i touch profits

profit + impact

everything i touch profits

profit + impact

everything i touch profits

profit + impact

everything i touch profits

profit + impact

everything i touch profits

profit + impact

everything i touch profits

profit + impact

everything i touch profits

profit + impact

everything i touch profits

profit + impact

everything i touch profits

profit + impact

everything i touch profits

profit + impact

everything i touch profits

profit + impact

everything i touch profits

profit + impact

everything i touch profits

profit + impact

everything i touch profits

profit + impact

everything i touch profits

profit + impact

everything i touch profits

profit + impact

everything i touch profits

profit + impact

everything i touch profits

profit + impact

everything i touch profits

profit + impact

everything i touch profits

profit + impact

everything i touch profits

profit + impact

everything i touch profits

profit + impact

everything i touch profits

profit + impact

everything i touch profits

profit + impact

everything i touch profits

profit + impact

everything i touch profits

profit + impact

everything i touch profits

profit + impact

everything i touch profits

profit + impact

everything i touch profits

profit + impact

everything i touch profits

profit + impact

everything i touch profits

profit + impact

everything i touch profits

profit + impact

everything i touch profits

profit + impact

everything i touch profits

profit + impact

everything i touch profits

profit + impact

everything i touch profits

profit + impact

everything i touch profits

profit + impact

everything i touch profits

profit + impact

everything i touch profits

profit + impact

everything i touch profits

profit + impact

everything i touch profits

profit + impact

everything i touch profits

profit + impact

everything i touch profits

profit + impact

everything i touch profits

profit + impact

everything i touch profits

profit + impact

everything i touch profits

profit + impact

everything i touch profits

profit + impact

everything i touch profits

profit + impact

everything i touch profits

profit + impact

everything i touch profits

profit + impact

everything i touch profits

profit + impact

everything i touch profits

profit + impact

everything i touch profits

profit + impact

everything i touch profits

profit + impact

everything i touch profits

profit + impact

everything i touch profits

profit + impact

everything i touch profits

profit + impact

everything i touch profits

profit + impact

everything i touch profits

profit + impact

everything i touch profits

profit + impact

everything i touch profits

profit + impact

everything i touch profits

profit + impact

everything i touch profits

profit + impact

everything i touch profits

profit + impact

everything i touch profits

profit + impact

everything i touch profits

profit + impact

everything i touch profits

profit + impact

everything i touch profits

profit + impact

everything i touch profits

profit + impact

everything i touch profits

profit + impact

everything i touch profits

profit + impact

everything i touch profits

profit + impact

everything i touch profits

profit + impact

everything i touch profits

profit + impact

everything i touch profits

profit + impact

everything i touch profits

profit + impact

everything i touch profits

profit + impact

everything i touch profits

profit + impact

everything i touch profits

profit + impact

everything i touch profits

profit + impact

everything i touch profits

profit + impact

everything i touch profits

profit + impact

everything i touch profits

profit + impact

everything i touch profits

profit + impact

everything i touch profits

profit + impact

everything i touch profits

profit + impact

everything i touch profits

profit + impact

everything i touch profits

profit + impact

everything i touch profits

profit + impact

everything i touch profits

i was created to be
EXTRAORDINARILY
profitable + impactful

www.ingramcontent.com/pod-product-compliance
Lightning Source LLC
Chambersburg PA
CBHW082203220526
45470CB00010B/3022